This book belongs to:

....
Name

....
Date

....

....

....

MARY
OF NAZARETH

THE LIFE OF OUR LADY IN PICTURES

FR. DONALD CALLOWAY, MIC
FOREWORD BY ALISSA JUNG

IGNATIUS

CONTENTS

FOREWORD

WHAT a wonderful book this is!

Looking at the amazing photos of *Mary of Nazareth*, I immediately travel back in my mind to Tunisia, in autumn 2011, where I had one of the most beautiful experiences of my life.

After a rather strange Internet audition in the summer of 2011, followed by a personal call to Rome to audition in person, I was chosen by Giacomo Campiotti to play the part of Mary in his movie *Mary of Nazareth.*

Initially I was extremely happy about this beautiful opportunity, but shortly afterward, I started to have doubts and questions: Am I able to do this big role? To represent a revered icon? How will I portray the Mother of Jesus? What if I'm not precise? What if I'm not able? What if . . . ?

But then, after this period of sinking feelings and self-doubts, I suddenly recognized and was inspired by the idea that I was not supposed to portray an untouchable icon, but rather to portray Mary as a real human being.

I understood that I had the chance to deeply empathize with a young girl who turned the world upside down by believing in something great that many around her did not. And to portray a Mother who had to let go of her only beloved Son for something very difficult, yet something she strongly believed in.

So I discovered the great beauty inside of Mary—her strength, her grace, her open mind, and her deep love.

Prepared with these thoughts, I started my trip to Tunisia where I had the most wonderful experience of shooting this movie with an international team of amazing colleagues. As seen in the movie, and as you will see revealed in the moving pictures in this book, it was an intense experience for all of us.

It was a very challenging project, working six days a week from 6:00 A.M. to 6:00 P.M., shooting with a huge international cast, hundreds of extras, six different languages on set, as well as camels, goats, and donkeys; having to cry three days in a row at Golgotha; wearing hot costumes in the sun with sand blowing in our eyes from the wind; and so on. But at the same time, we had a most wonderful and profound experience, full of unique and deep human relations. We were like a family.

I am very grateful to have had the honor of shooting this movie and portraying Mary, the Mother of Jesus.

I truly hope that, by reading this book and looking at these beautiful pictures, you will also experience the depth and beauty of this profound story of Mary of Nazareth.

Alissa Jung

EARLY LIFE of MARY

"This grand princess [Mary] is the honor and perfection of all in the order of nature, since in her and by her the Creator of the world has united himself to man."

—St. John Eudes

"Mary is the most loved and loving Daughter of God the Father."

—Blessed Gabriele
Maria Allegra

"Mary was a princess of God, and God gave her the best blood of Israel."

—Servant of God
Patrick J. Peyton

MARY is the masterpiece of God! She is his perfect creation and his most beloved daughter. She is the Immaculata!

Preserved from all sin, she has been given every grace and blessing in order to grow and become the Mother of the Messiah, the Mother of the God-man.

The Blessed Virgin Mary is, indeed, the most lovely girl who ever existed.

She was a tender little girl with a feminine heart, an immaculate, feminine heart that longed to dwell in the house of her heavenly Father. She is full of grace and has the plentitude of feminine wonder. Daddy's little girl is a beautiful princess, and the heavenly Father delights in the delicate femininity of his most beloved daughter. She is, in fact, the most painted woman in the history of the world.

And for her part, little Mary knows that the heavenly Father loves her. She is his little princess, his sweetheart, the joy of his heart, and the apple of his eye.

Many of the saints and mystics who have written about the hidden life of little Mary have depicted the heavenly Father's little princess on the day she was presented in the Temple by her parents, Saints Joachim and Anne, as dancing on the steps of the Temple in Jerusalem. She danced out of pure joy for her heavenly Father!

Throughout the centuries, many artists have depicted this beautiful event through Christian art, and these artistic renditions can be found in museums around the world.

"She [Mary] holds all the great Truths of Christianity together, as a piece of wood holds a kite. Children wrap the string of a kite around a stick and release the string as the kite climbs to the heavens. Mary is like that piece of wood. Around her we wrap all the precious strings of the great Truths of our holy Faith—for example, the Incarnation, the Eucharist, the Church. No matter how far we get above the earth, as the kite may, we always have need of Mary to hold the doctrines of the Creed together. If we threw away the stick, we would no longer have the kite; if we threw away Mary, we would never have Our Lord. He would be lost in the Heavens, like our runaway kite, and that would be terrible, indeed, for us on earth."

—Venerable Fulton J. Sheen

IN THE beginning of time, God made a garden for Adam and Eve. It was created for them to be a delight and a place to converse with God.

In the new creation and covenant, the New Adam, Jesus Christ, has created a more perfect garden, in which he invites all people to take delight, for this garden serves as a place to encounter his true presence.

This garden is none other than his most loving Mother. She is the New Eve and the Mother of all the living.

THE Blessed Virgin Mary is a perpetual virgin. Her womb is a sanctuary made for God alone.

As light passes through a window and does not compromise the integrity of the glass, so the Son of God who is Light from Light, true God from true God, would come into the world through the virginal womb of Mary.

As dew passes through a flower and yet leaves the integrity of the flower intact, so the Messiah was to enter into the world.

"In the sixth month the angel Gabriel was sent from God to a city of Galilee named Nazareth, to a virgin betrothed to a man whose name was Joseph, of the house of David; and the virgin's name was Mary. And he came to her and said, 'Hail, full of grace, the Lord is with you!'"

—Luke 1:26–28

W HEN Mary journeys in haste to visit her relative Elizabeth and her husband, Zechariah, she does not go alone.

She is now the tabernacle of the Most High and the ark of the true presence of God.

And where Jesus and Mary are present, there is joy, and the mute are able to speak!

"My soul magnifies the Lord, and my spirit rejoices in God my Savior, for he has regarded the low estate of his handmaiden.

For behold, henceforth all generations will call me blessed; for he who is mighty has done great things for me, and holy is his name.

And his mercy is on those who fear him from generation to generation.

He has shown the strength of his arm, he has scattered
the proud in the imagination of their hearts,
and exalted those of low degree;
he has filled the hungry with
good things, and the
rich he has sent
empty away.

He has helped his servant Israel, in remembrance
of his mercy, as he spoke to our fathers,
to Abraham and to his posterity
forever."

—Luke 1:46–55

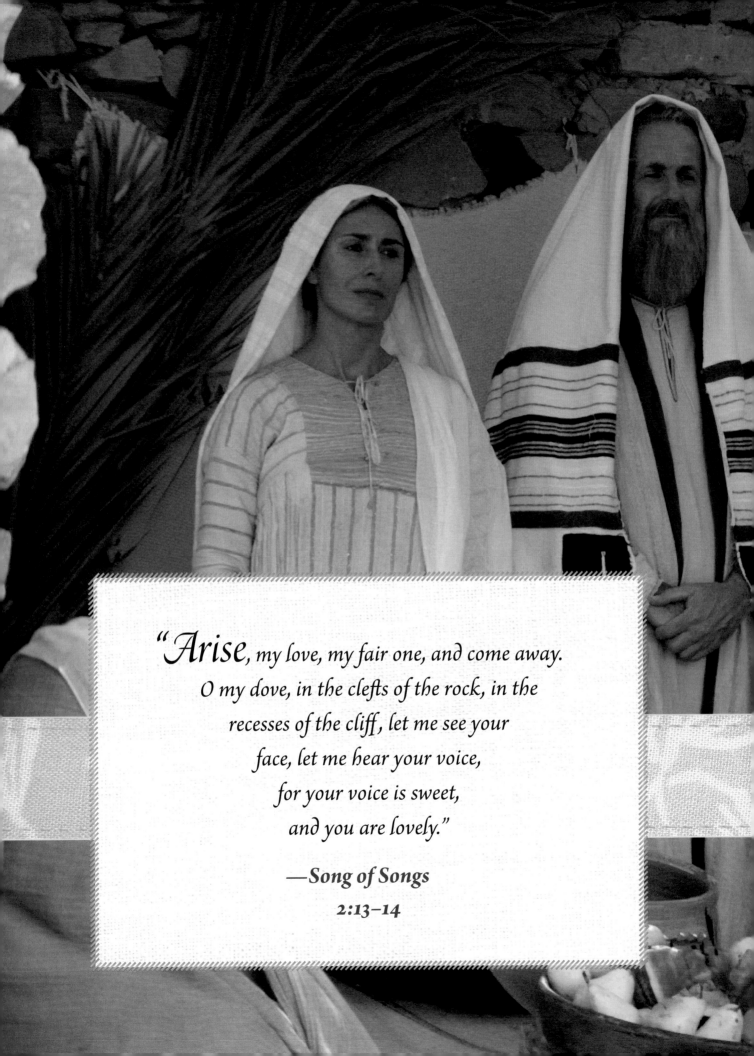

"*Arise*, my love, my fair one, and come away.
O my dove, in the clefts of the rock, in the
recesses of the cliff, let me see your
face, let me hear your voice,
for your voice is sweet,
and you are lovely."

—Song of Songs

2:13–14

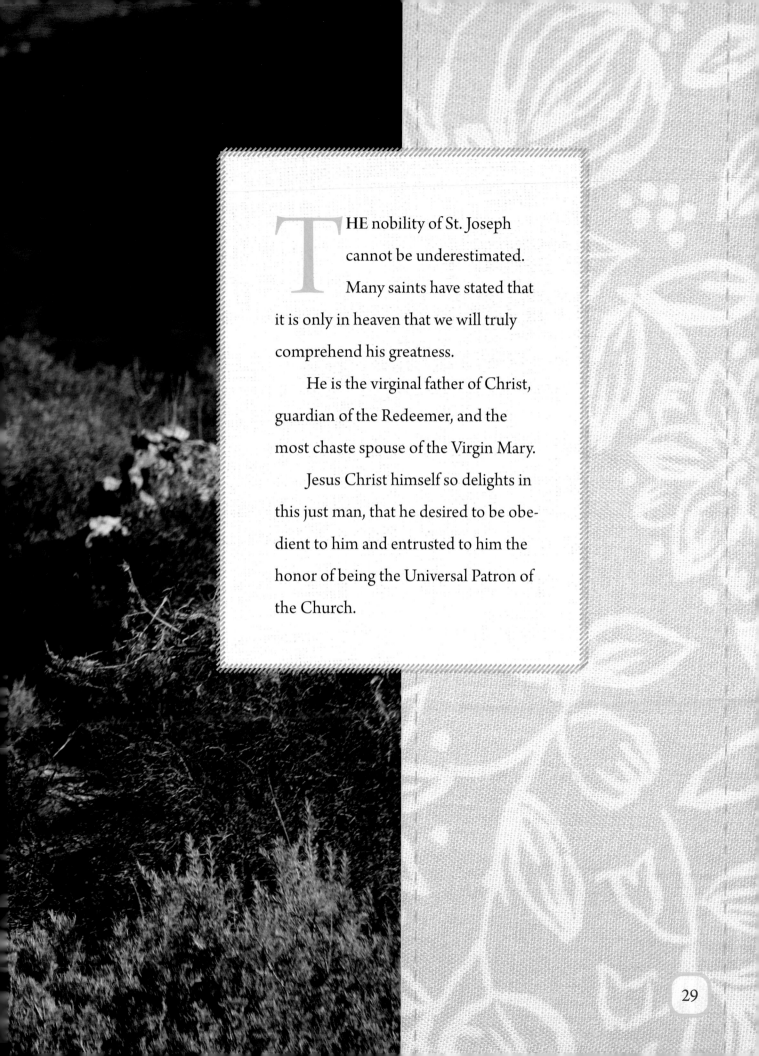

THE nobility of St. Joseph cannot be underestimated. Many saints have stated that it is only in heaven that we will truly comprehend his greatness.

He is the virginal father of Christ, guardian of the Redeemer, and the most chaste spouse of the Virgin Mary.

Jesus Christ himself so delights in this just man, that he desired to be obedient to him and entrusted to him the honor of being the Universal Patron of the Church.

COMING of the SAVIOR

"Behold, 'the mother of Jesus,' mother immaculate, mother untouched, mother who never experienced the pains of motherhood, mother uncorrupt, mother not deprived of the virtue of virginal chastity. She is spotless, a fitting mother for the spotless Lamb."

—St. Albert the Great

"The Infant Jesus doesn't preach, or perform any miracles; he just receives the sweet caresses of his dearest mother because that is the will of his Father, who is in heaven."

—Servant of God
Mother Auxilia de la Cruz

"Among creatures no one knows Christ better than Mary; no one can introduce us to a profound knowledge of his mystery better than his mother."

—St. John Paul II

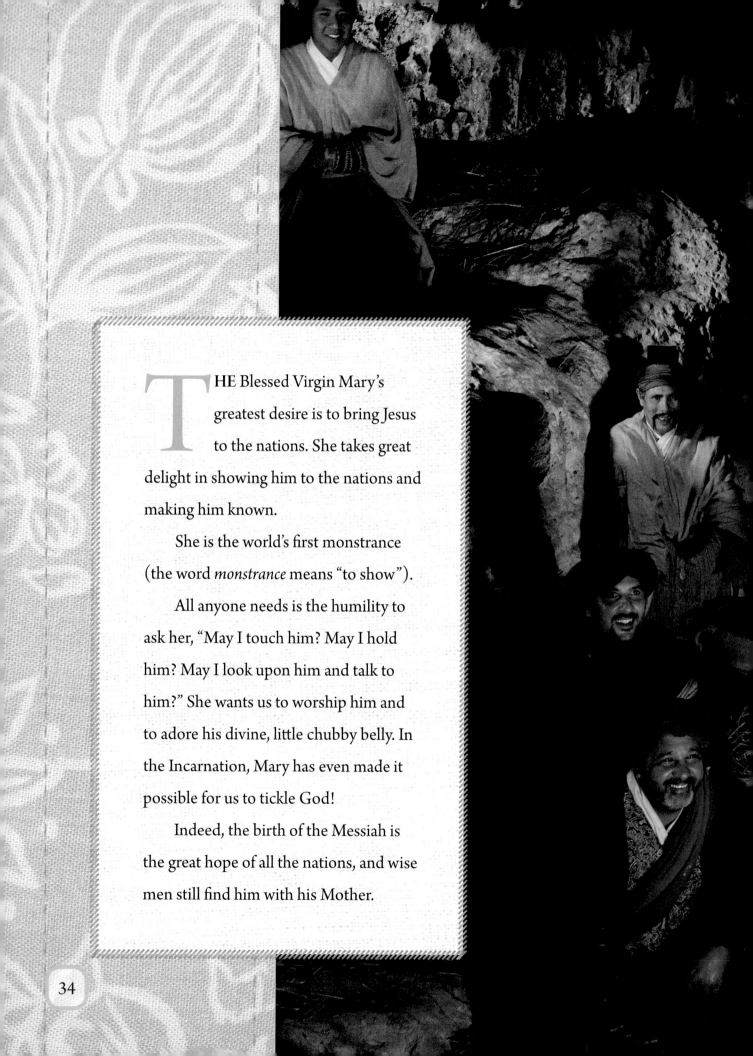

THE Blessed Virgin Mary's greatest desire is to bring Jesus to the nations. She takes great delight in showing him to the nations and making him known.

She is the world's first monstrance (the word *monstrance* means "to show").

All anyone needs is the humility to ask her, "May I touch him? May I hold him? May I look upon him and talk to him?" She wants us to worship him and to adore his divine, little chubby belly. In the Incarnation, Mary has even made it possible for us to tickle God!

Indeed, the birth of the Messiah is the great hope of all the nations, and wise men still find him with his Mother.

"Was he [St. Joseph] old or young? Most of the statues and pictures we see of Joseph today represent him as an old man with a gray beard, one who took Mary and her vow [of virginity] under his protection with somewhat the same detachment as a doctor would pick up a baby girl in a nursery. We have, of course, no historical evidence whatever concerning the age of Joseph. Some apocryphal accounts picture him as an old man; Fathers of the Church, after the fourth century, followed this legend rather rigidly. . . .

"But when one searches for the reasons why Christian art should have pictured Joseph as aged, we discover that it was in order better to safeguard the virginity of Mary. Somehow, the assumption had crept in that senility was a better protector of virginity than adolescence. Art thus unconsciously made Joseph a spouse chaste and pure by age rather than by virtue. But this is like assuming that the best way to show that a man would never steal is to picture him without hands. . . .

"But more than that, to make Joseph out as old portrays for us a man who had little vital energy left, rather than one who, having it, kept it in chains for God's sake and for his holy purposes. To make Joseph appear pure only because his flesh had aged is like glorifying a mountain stream that has dried. . . .

"Joseph was probably a young man, strong, virile, athletic, handsome, chaste, and disciplined."

—**Venerable Fulton J. Sheen**

FAMILY is the fundamental basis of society. God established it this way, and when he desired to take on human flesh and become incarnate, he entered the world through a family, the Holy Family.

It has been said by many saints that the Holy Family is like an earthly Trinity and serves as an icon of the Holy Trinity in heaven. The communion of love that existed in the home of Joseph and Mary at Nazareth truly serves as the model for all human families. Love, sacrifice, prayer, and hard work were the hallmarks of the lives of Jesus, Mary, and Joseph.

Never have four walls and a roof seen such purity and holiness! The very walls of their humble home are relics worthy of veneration!

In their poverty, they were rich. In their lowliness, they were exalted. In their familial love, they were filled with joy!

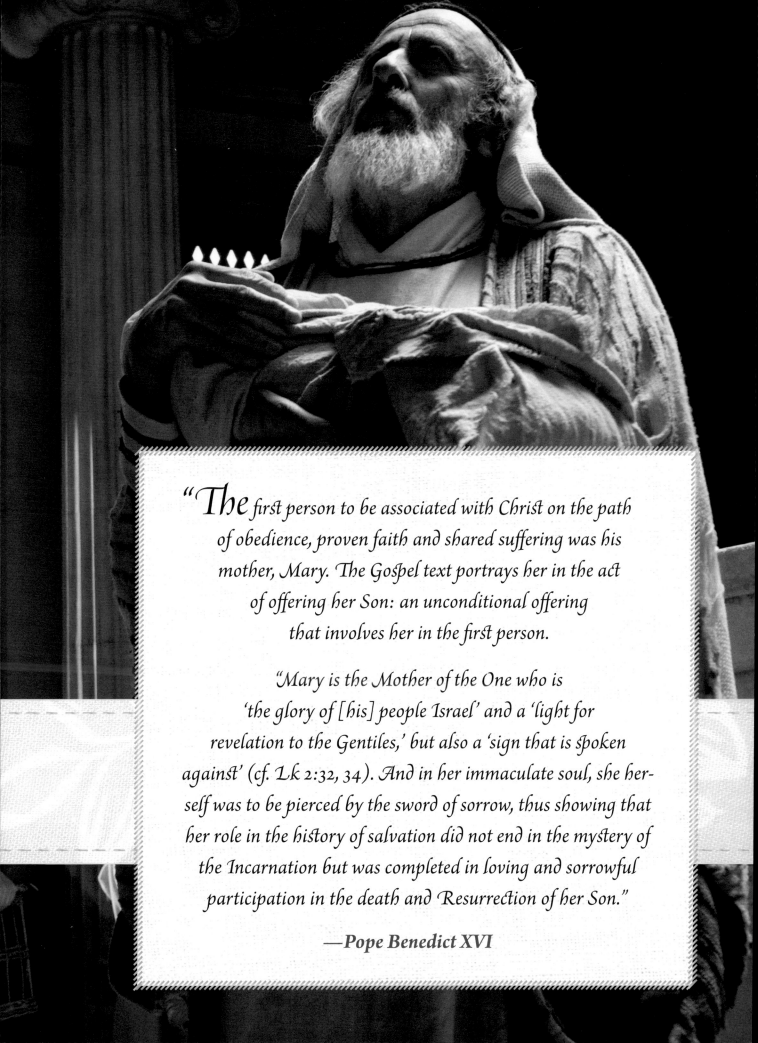

"The first person to be associated with Christ on the path of obedience, proven faith and shared suffering was his mother, Mary. The Gospel text portrays her in the act of offering her Son: an unconditional offering that involves her in the first person.

"Mary is the Mother of the One who is 'the glory of [his] people Israel' and a 'light for revelation to the Gentiles,' but also a 'sign that is spoken against' (cf. Lk 2:32, 34). And in her immaculate soul, she herself was to be pierced by the sword of sorrow, thus showing that her role in the history of salvation did not end in the mystery of the Incarnation but was completed in loving and sorrowful participation in the death and Resurrection of her Son."

—Pope Benedict XVI

"Now there was a man in Jerusalem, whose name
was Simeon, and this man was righteous and devout,
looking for the consolation of Israel, and the Holy
Spirit was upon him. And it had been revealed to
him by the Holy Spirit that he should not see
death before he had seen the Lord's Christ.
And inspired by the Spirit he came into
the temple; and when the parents
brought in the child Jesus,
to do for him according
to the custom of the law,
he took him up in his arms
and blessed God and said, "'Lord,
now let your servant depart in peace,
according to your word; for my eyes have
seen your salvation which you have prepared
in the presence of all peoples, a light for revelation
to the Gentiles, and for glory to your people Israel.'
"And his father and his mother marveled at what was said
about him; and Simeon blessed them and said to Mary his
mother, "'Behold this child is set for the fall and rising of many
in Israel, and for a sign that is spoken against (and a sword will
pierce through your own soul also), that thoughts out of many
hearts may be revealed.'"

—Luke 2:25–35

PLEASURES and comforts of the world are fleeting. They are here today, and gone tomorrow.

Jesus Christ, the Son of God and the Son of Mary, came to set us free from our bondage to sin. The mercy of God is for everyone, and Our Lady, as Mary Magdalene will discover in her own life, is the gateway to Jesus.

As the aqueduct of grace and the Mother of Divine Mercy, Mary always leads sinners to Jesus and his offer of salvation.

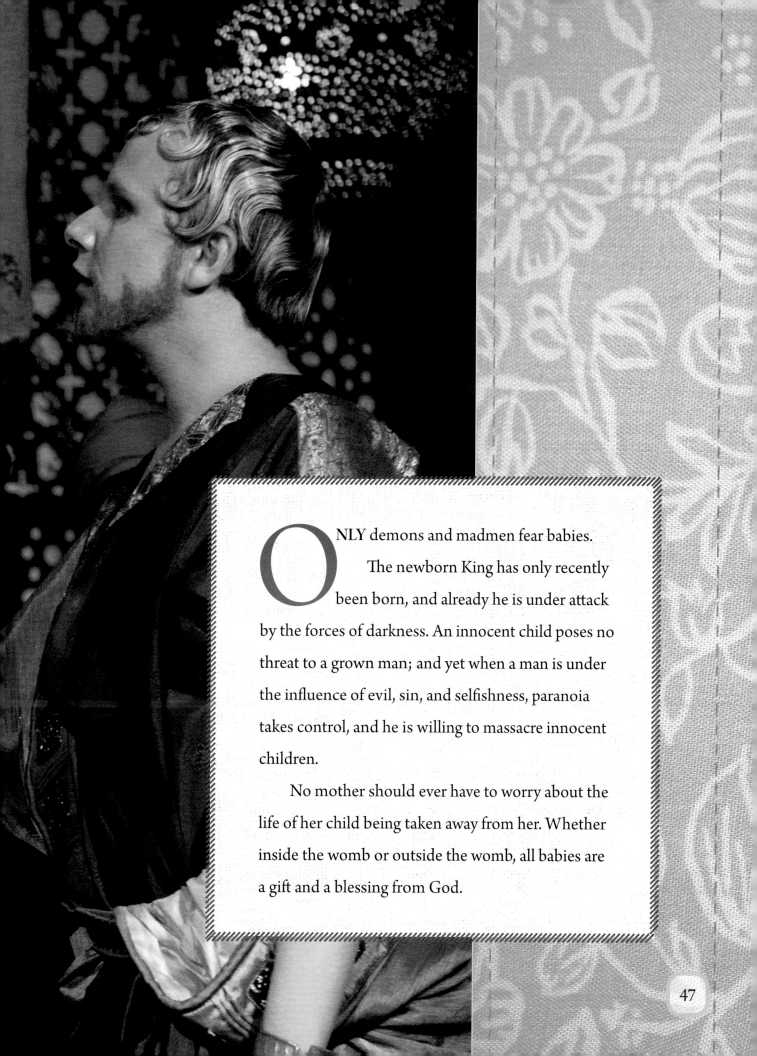

ONLY demons and madmen fear babies. The newborn King has only recently been born, and already he is under attack by the forces of darkness. An innocent child poses no threat to a grown man; and yet when a man is under the influence of evil, sin, and selfishness, paranoia takes control, and he is willing to massacre innocent children.

No mother should ever have to worry about the life of her child being taken away from her. Whether inside the womb or outside the womb, all babies are a gift and a blessing from God.

"**Behold**, an angel of the Lord appeared to Joseph in a dream and said, 'Rise, take the child and his mother, and flee to Egypt, and remain there till I tell you; for Herod is about to search for the child, to destroy him.'

"And he rose and took the child and his mother by night, and departed to Egypt, and remained there until the death of Herod."

—Matthew 2:13–15

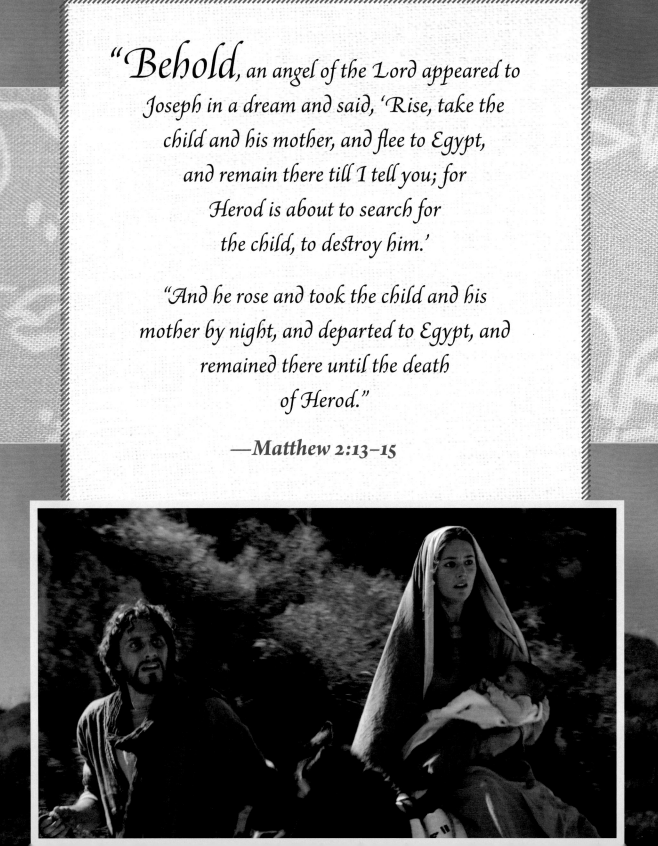

"*He* [Jesus] *became man of her; and received her lineaments and her features as the appearance and character under which he should manifest himself to the world. He was known, doubtless, by this likeness to be her Son. Thus his mother is the first of the Prophets, for, of her, came the Word bodily; she is the sole oracle of Truth, for the Way, the Truth, and the Life vouchsafed to be her Son; she is the one mold of Divine Wisdom, and in that mold it was indelibly set.*"

**—Blessed
John Henry Newman**

JESUS loves his Mother so much that during his life on this earth he dedicated thirty hidden years to Mary, while he only shared three public years with his disciples. This means he gave ten times as much of his life to her in the home of Nazareth.

And what did they do during those thirty years? They prayed, worked, played, and enjoyed the sweet company of each other's presence.

It can be said that during those thirty years, Mary was in an almost constant state of adoration, for every day she beheld God in the flesh and adored him, worshipped him, fed him, kissed him, and sang him to sleep with a lullaby.

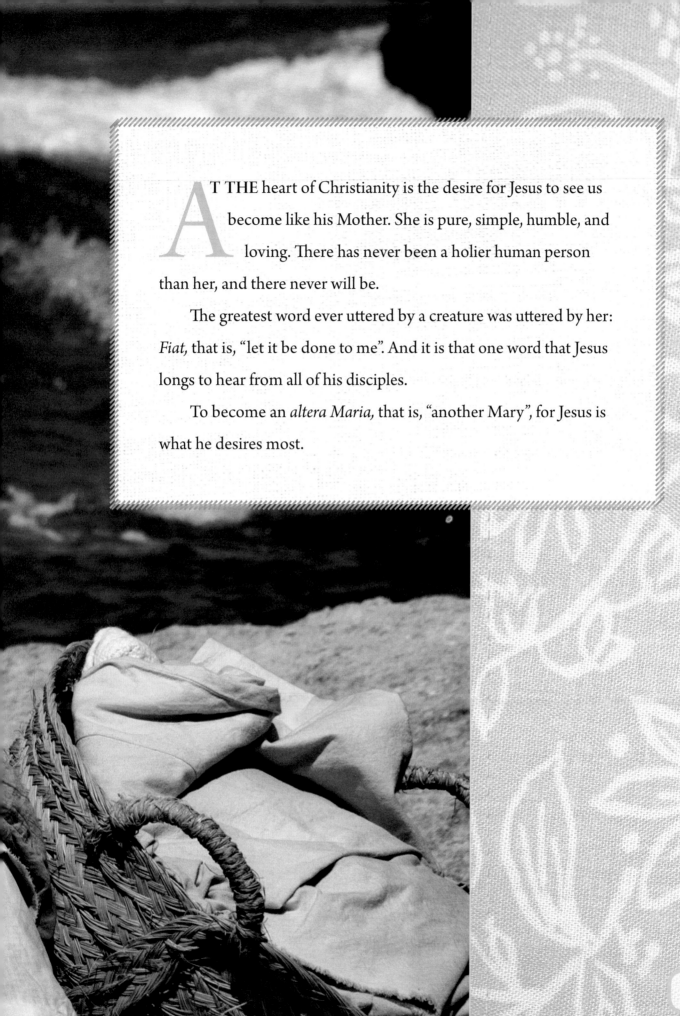

AT THE heart of Christianity is the desire for Jesus to see us become like his Mother. She is pure, simple, humble, and loving. There has never been a holier human person than her, and there never will be.

The greatest word ever uttered by a creature was uttered by her: *Fiat,* that is, "let it be done to me". And it is that one word that Jesus longs to hear from all of his disciples.

To become an *altera Maria,* that is, "another Mary", for Jesus is what he desires most.

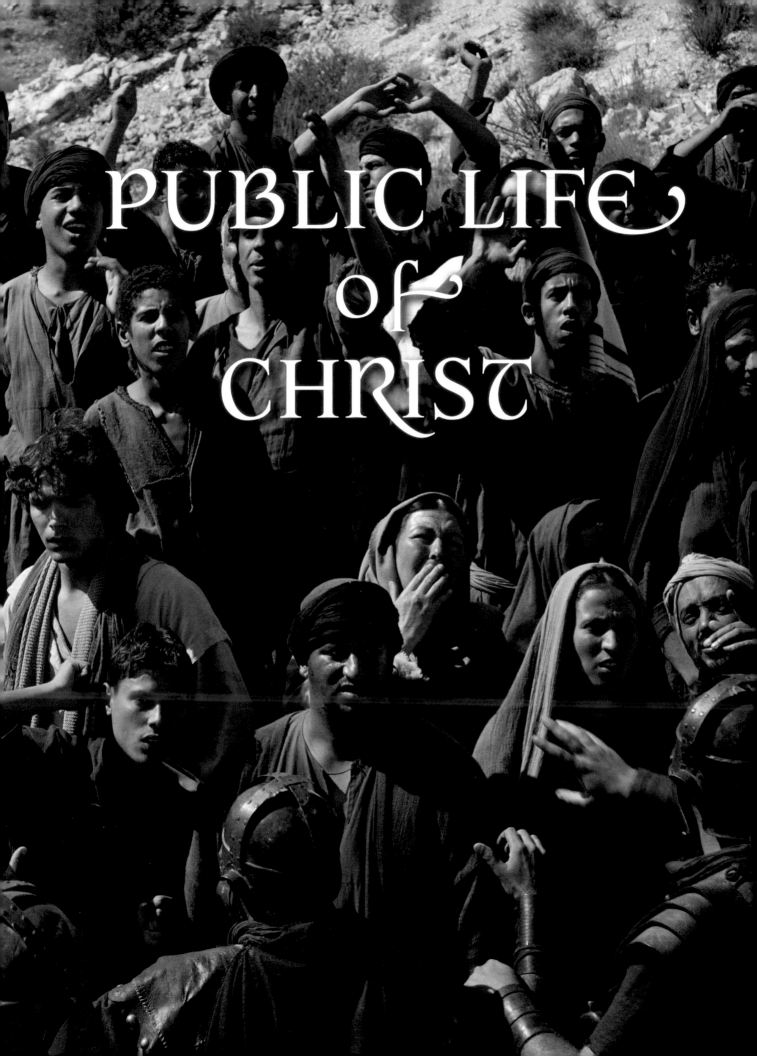

PUBLIC LIFE of CHRIST

THE first miracle that Jesus does in his public ministry is to turn 180 gallons of water into wine! And this miracle is done through the intercession of his Mother.

Though she is a creature, she is also his Mother, and her words have power.

And as a faithful and loving Son, Jesus hears her maternal request and fulfills it as if it were a gentle command. It greatly pleases the heart of Christ to bring joy to the heart of his Mother.

"She [Mary] sees and understands the difficulty of
the young married couple at whose wedding feast
the wine runs out; she thinks about it, she
knows that Jesus can do something
and decides to address her Son
so that he may intervene."

—Pope Francis

WHEN he was in the womb of his mother, St. John the Baptist leapt for joy when his mother heard the sound of Mary's voice, for Mary carried in her womb the Lamb of God who came to take away the sins of the world.

Now, as a grown man and "prophet of the Most High", he once again draws attention to the Lamb of God by calling all sinners to repentance and conversion.

" 'Let not your hearts be troubled; believe in God,
believe also in me. In my Father's house are many
rooms; if it were not so, would I have told you
that I go to prepare a place for you? And
when I go and prepare a place for you,
I will come again and will take you
to myself, that where I am you
may be also. And you
know the way
where I am
going.'

"Thomas said to him,
'Lord, we do not know where you are going; how can
we know the way?'

"Jesus said to him,
'I am the way, and the truth,
and the life; no one comes to the Father,
but by me. If you had known me, you would have
known my Father also; henceforth you know him and
have seen him.'"

—*John 14:1–7*

"**On** Mary's motherly face Christians recognize a most particular expression of the merciful love of God, who with the mediation of a maternal presence has us better understand the Father's own care and goodness.

"Mary appears as the one who attracts sinners and reveals to them, with her sympathy and her indulgence, the divine offer of reconciliation."

—St. John Paul II

HOW sad it is that, when Jesus returned to his hometown of Nazareth and spoke in the synagogue, he was kicked out of town and even threatened to be killed by being thrown off the brow of the hill (see Lk 4:16–30).

Undoubtedly, since it was his hometown, Mary would have been there and witnessed all of this. How her maternal heart must have suffered as she watched her divine Son be rejected and ridiculed by the very people he grew up with. These were his neighbors; these were his childhood friends!

"The Virgin Mary herself, among all human creatures the closest to God, still had to walk day after day on a pilgrimage of faith, constantly guarding and meditating in her heart on the Word that God addressed to her through the HolyScripture and through the events of the life of her Son, in whom she recognized and welcomed the Lord's mysterious voice."

—**Pope Benedict XVI**

THE human heart was made for happiness. Nothing will ever totally satisfy our desire for happiness until we surrender our lives to God. And there will be times in all of our lives when we will hear the truth spoken to us. It will be a time of grace, a time of conversion, and a time of mercy. In order to respond to this grace, we need to have a humble heart and a trusting spirit.

God offers an ocean of mercy for the sinner. All that we need in order to respond are humility and trust.

The Virgin Mary is always there to help us find our way to Jesus, assuring us that no matter what we have done, the mercy of God is greater than our sin.

"If Mary and Martha's tears compelled Christ to raise their dead brother from the tomb, what sin can be so strong, that the power of Divine Mercy cannot extinguish it through the intercession of the Virgin Mother?"

—St. Anselm of Lucca

"The moment of conversion is not the same for all. St. Augustine, St. Mary of Egypt and many others spent a considerable part of their lives far from God, while others were ravished by grace from the very beginning. But however we are converted, the Mother of Mercy is always the instrumental cause, for, by God's will, no grace is given to us but through the mediation of the Immaculate Heart of Mary."

—Blessed Michael Sopocko

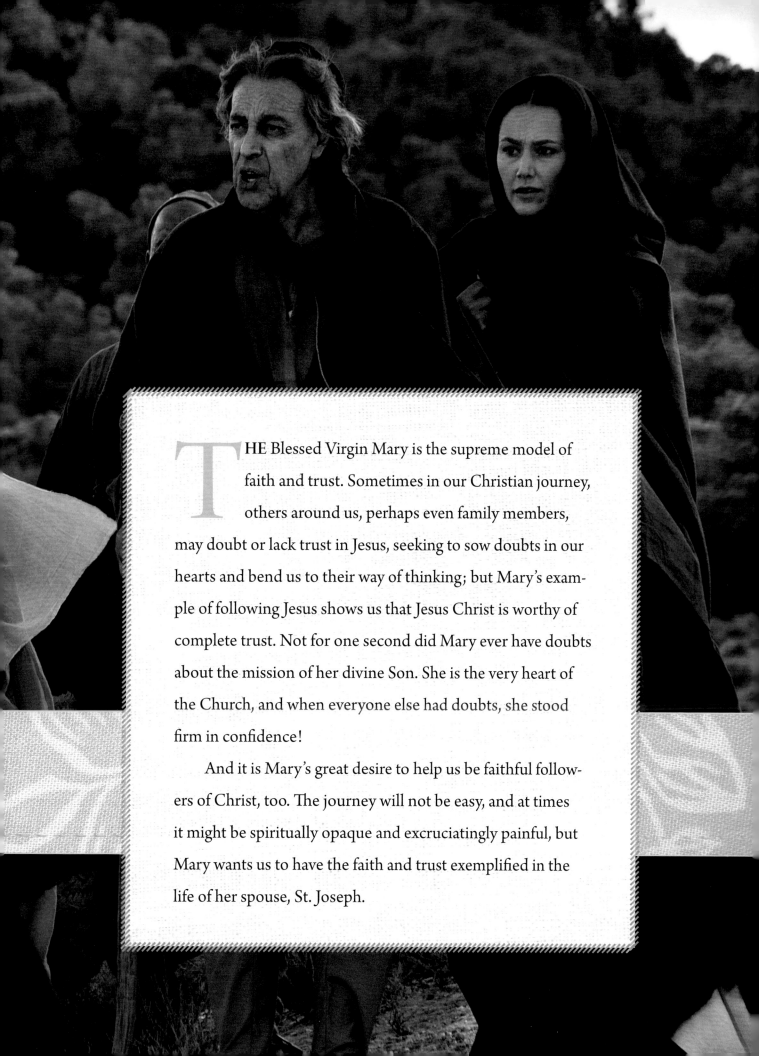

THE Blessed Virgin Mary is the supreme model of faith and trust. Sometimes in our Christian journey, others around us, perhaps even family members, may doubt or lack trust in Jesus, seeking to sow doubts in our hearts and bend us to their way of thinking; but Mary's example of following Jesus shows us that Jesus Christ is worthy of complete trust. Not for one second did Mary ever have doubts about the mission of her divine Son. She is the very heart of the Church, and when everyone else had doubts, she stood firm in confidence!

And it is Mary's great desire to help us be faithful followers of Christ, too. The journey will not be easy, and at times it might be spiritually opaque and excruciatingly painful, but Mary wants us to have the faith and trust exemplified in the life of her spouse, St. Joseph.

"Mary is the depository of all graces,
but who can better induce her to open
the celestial treasury than Joseph,
her glorious spouse?

"A servant of Mary will
therefore have a
tender
devotion to
St. Joseph,
and by
his pious
homage of respect
and love, will endeavor to
merit the protection of this great saint.

"He will beg of him the grace of dying as he himself did,
with the kiss of Jesus and in the arms of Mary."

—Blessed
William Joseph Chaminade

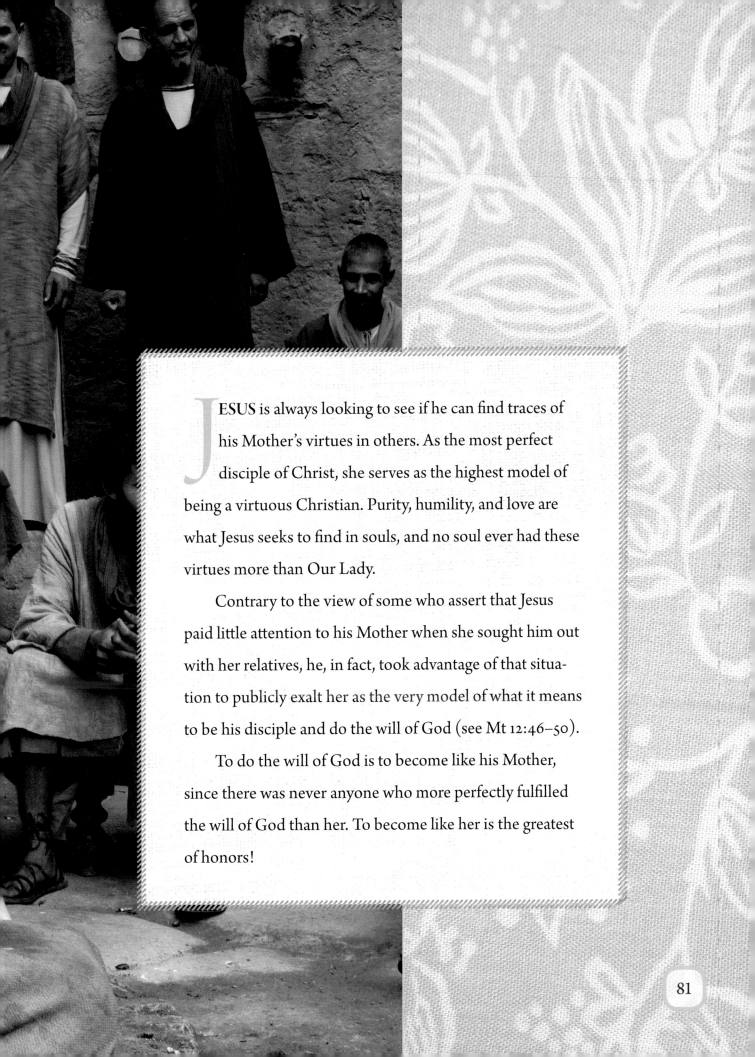

JESUS is always looking to see if he can find traces of his Mother's virtues in others. As the most perfect disciple of Christ, she serves as the highest model of being a virtuous Christian. Purity, humility, and love are what Jesus seeks to find in souls, and no soul ever had these virtues more than Our Lady.

Contrary to the view of some who assert that Jesus paid little attention to his Mother when she sought him out with her relatives, he, in fact, took advantage of that situation to publicly exalt her as the very model of what it means to be his disciple and do the will of God (see Mt 12:46–50).

To do the will of God is to become like his Mother, since there was never anyone who more perfectly fulfilled the will of God than her. To become like her is the greatest of honors!

"THE reason why Mary became his mother and why he did not come
sooner was that she alone, and no creature before her or after her,
was the pure Vessel of Grace, promised by God to mankind
as the Mother of the Incarnate Word, by the merits
of whose Passion mankind was to be redeemed
from its guilt.

"The Blessed Virgin was the one and
only pure blossom of the human
race, flowering in the
fullness of time."

—Blessed
Anne Catherine Emmerich

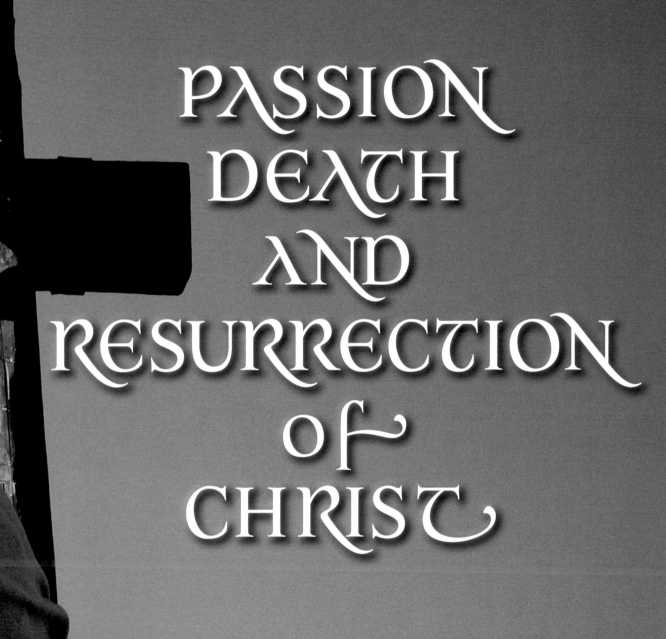

PASSION DEATH AND RESURRECTION OF CHRIST

"*And* he came out [of the Upper Room], and went, as was his custom, to the Mount of Olives; and the disciples followed him. "And when he came to the place he said to them, 'Pray that you may not enter into temptation.' "And he withdrew from them about a stone's throw, and knelt down and prayed, 'Father, if you are willing, remove this chalice from me; nevertheless not my will, but yours, be done.'

"And there
appeared to him
an angel from heaven,
strengthening
him.

"And being in an agony he prayed
more earnestly; and his sweat became like
great drops of blood falling down upon the ground."

—Luke 22:39–44

JESUS Christ, Divine Mercy incarnate, allows himself to be taken into captivity out of love for us. He is our merciful High Priest. And nobody knows the depths of God's love and mercy more than the Virgin Mary.

So great was God's love for Mary that in anticipation of Christ's merits on the Cross, God the Father had already freely given her the privilege of being the Immaculate Conception, a prevenient mercy that flows from the sacrificial Cross of his divine Son. Therefore, because of the gift of her Immaculate Conception, Jesus must die for her, since she has already received the plentitude of his mercy by having been conceived without original sin.

And so now Jesus begins his Via Dolorosa (Way of Suffering) to manifest to the world the immense love he has for his Immaculate Mother. And he goes to die for all of us, so that we, too, can be recipients of his Divine Mercy and share eternal life with him in heaven.

"*As* one cannot go to a statue of a mother holding a child and cut away the mother without destroying the child, so neither can one have Jesus without his Mother. Could you claim as a friend one who, every time he came into your home, refused to speak to your mother or treated her with cold indifference? Jesus cannot feel pleased with those who never give recognition to or show respect for his mother. Coldness to his mother is certainly not the best way to keep warm a friendship with him. The unkindest cut of all would be to say that she who is the mother of our Lord is unworthy of being our mother."

—*Venerable*
Fulton J. Sheen

ACCORDING to God's holy Word, the bookends of human history are about God, *through the chosen woman,* crushing the serpent (see Gen 3:15; Rev 12). This *chosen woman* is the Blessed Virgin Mary.

She is not God, but she is the chosen vessel of the Messiah. As a creature she does not possess the power to crush the serpent, but God has chosen to live in her, and therefore they together crush the serpent's head. God willed it to happen this way.

God knows this because he set it up this way, the saints know this because they found protection and victory under the mantle of the *chosen woman,* and Satan knows it, too, because he knows whose foot it is that crushes his head.

And this is why the devil strives to *dis-mantle* Christianity, that is, to separate souls from having a love and devotion to the *chosen woman,* Mary.

Under the mantle of Mary we are safe. When Mary is not present in a person's life, the devil perceives no threat. But where Mary is present, Christ is truly present, and the darkness will be crushed and the victory guaranteed!

"Oh, what great sorrow it must have been for the mother, after Jesus was born, to think that they had to then crucify him! What pangs she must have always had in her heart! How many sighs she must have made, and how many times she must have wept! Yet she never complained."

—St. Gemma Galgani

"She [Mary] participated in the same torments, not by way of the executioners, like Jesus, but she, by way of love and sorrow, participated in all the torments, one by one. The heart of Jesus and the heart of Mary both stood united in suffering and in love, and this they offered to God the Father for all of us."

—St. Veronica Giuliani

"The sword that Christ ran into his own heart and Mary's soul has become so blunted by the pressings that it can never wound so fiercely again."

—Venerable Fulton J. Sheen

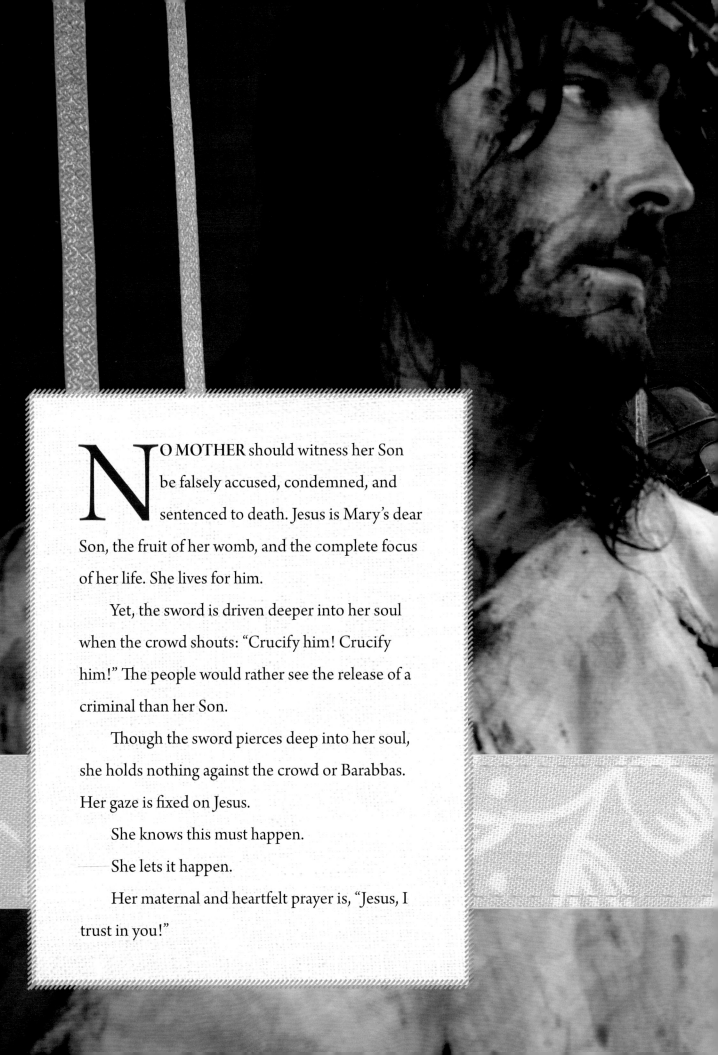

NO MOTHER should witness her Son be falsely accused, condemned, and sentenced to death. Jesus is Mary's dear Son, the fruit of her womb, and the complete focus of her life. She lives for him.

Yet, the sword is driven deeper into her soul when the crowd shouts: "Crucify him! Crucify him!" The people would rather see the release of a criminal than her Son.

Though the sword pierces deep into her soul, she holds nothing against the crowd or Barabbas. Her gaze is fixed on Jesus.

She knows this must happen.

She lets it happen.

Her maternal and heartfelt prayer is, "Jesus, I trust in you!"

"*If you do not understand Our Lady, you do not understand Christianity, because Christianity puts her in a most extraordinary position.*"

—**Servant of God**
Frank Duff

"*If Peter, from the fact that, by divine revelation, he professed Christ as the true Son of God and the Messiah, merited to be called blessed and to be made Christ's vicar, the rock of the Church and the keeper of the keys, what must we say of Mary?*"

—**St. Lawrence of Brindisi**

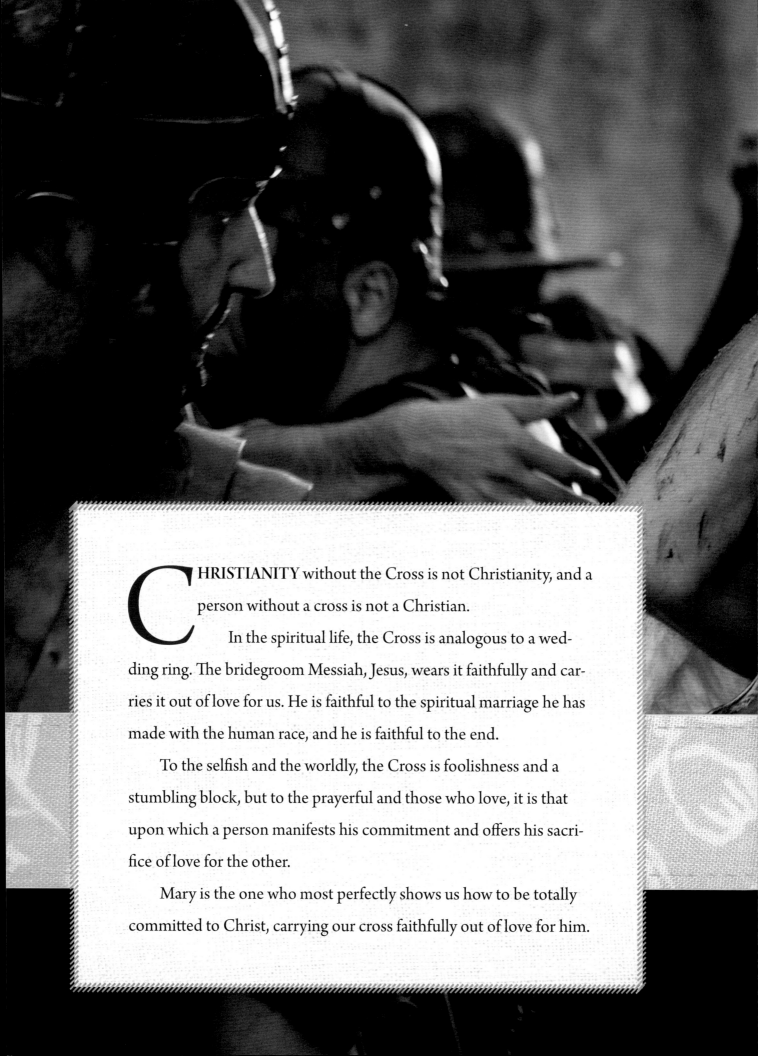

CHRISTIANITY without the Cross is not Christianity, and a person without a cross is not a Christian.

In the spiritual life, the Cross is analogous to a wedding ring. The bridegroom Messiah, Jesus, wears it faithfully and carries it out of love for us. He is faithful to the spiritual marriage he has made with the human race, and he is faithful to the end.

To the selfish and the worldly, the Cross is foolishness and a stumbling block, but to the prayerful and those who love, it is that upon which a person manifests his commitment and offers his sacrifice of love for the other.

Mary is the one who most perfectly shows us how to be totally committed to Christ, carrying our cross faithfully out of love for him.

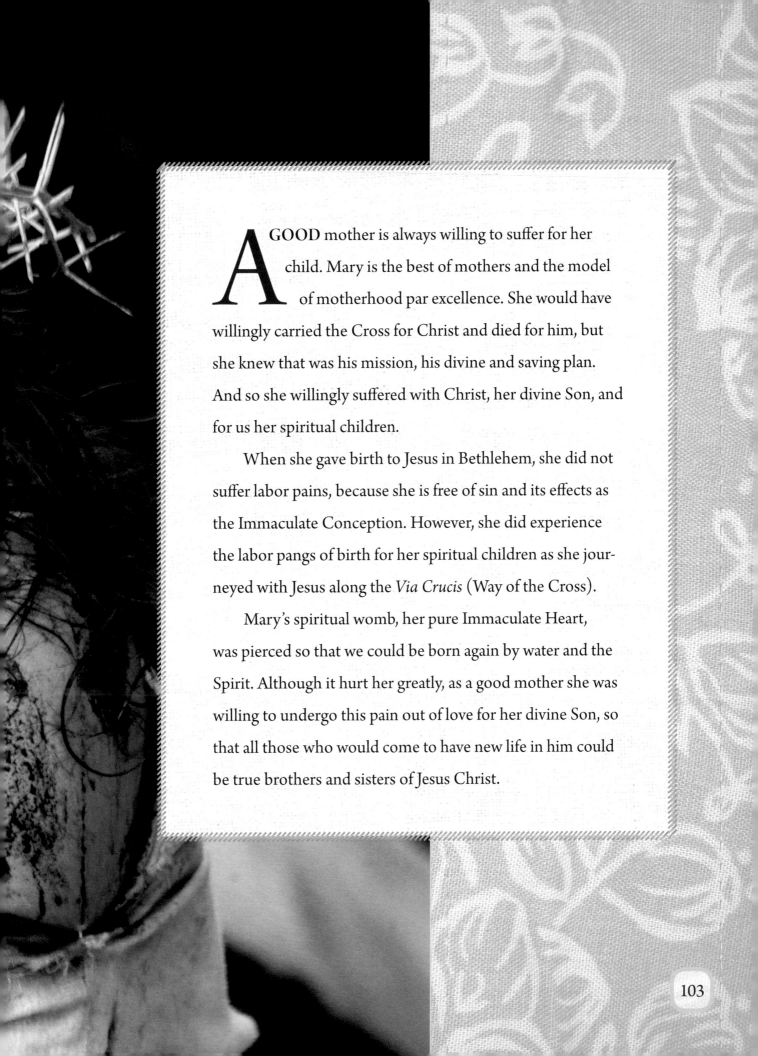

A GOOD mother is always willing to suffer for her child. Mary is the best of mothers and the model of motherhood par excellence. She would have willingly carried the Cross for Christ and died for him, but she knew that was his mission, his divine and saving plan. And so she willingly suffered with Christ, her divine Son, and for us her spiritual children.

When she gave birth to Jesus in Bethlehem, she did not suffer labor pains, because she is free of sin and its effects as the Immaculate Conception. However, she did experience the labor pangs of birth for her spiritual children as she journeyed with Jesus along the *Via Crucis* (Way of the Cross).

Mary's spiritual womb, her pure Immaculate Heart, was pierced so that we could be born again by water and the Spirit. Although it hurt her greatly, as a good mother she was willing to undergo this pain out of love for her divine Son, so that all those who would come to have new life in him could be true brothers and sisters of Jesus Christ.

"*Never* be afraid of loving the Blessed Virgin too much. You can never love her more than Jesus did."

—St. Maximilian Kolbe

"*Have* no fear of loving the Blessed Virgin too much; you will never love her enough, and Jesus will be pleased since the Blessed Virgin is his mother."

—St. Thérèse of Lisieux

JESUS reigns from the Cross. He is the King of glory, and as King he pours gifts on his people from his throne.

The night before he died, he gave his disciples the greatest gift he could ever give, his very own Body and Blood (the Holy Eucharist), instituted as the ongoing and living memorial of his everlasting love.

And now from the throne of the Cross, when consummating his sacrificial love by offering the Eternal Father his body, blood, soul, and divinity for the salvation of the world, he continues to give gifts to his people. He gives his own Mother to be our Mother! Without her he would not have had his flesh and blood to offer to his Father for the life of the world. Therefore, like the Eucharist, the gift of Mary's motherhood is a gift he desires everyone to have!

"Standing by the cross of Jesus were his mother, and his mother's sister, Mary the wife of Clopas, and Mary Magdalene. When Jesus saw his mother, and the disciple whom he loved standing near, he said to his mother, 'Woman, behold, your son!' Then he said to the disciple, 'Behold, your mother!' And from that hour the disciple took her to his own home."

—John 19: 25–27

"She [Mary] knew her office and her mission: she accomplished these most faithfully, even to the very end, by cooperating with the Son as Co-Redemptrix ."

—Blessed
James Alberione

"Mary is our Co-Redemptrix with Jesus. She gave Jesus his body and suffered with him at the foot of the Cross."

—Blessed
Teresa of Calcutta

"From the nature of his work the Redeemer ought to have associated his mother with his work. For this reason we invoke her under the title of Co-Redemptrix. She gave us the Savior, she accompanied him in the work of redemption as far as the Cross itself, sharing with him the sorrows of the agony and of the death in which Jesus consummated the redemption of mankind."

—Pope Pius XI

"**Where** Mary is, there is the archetype of total self-giving and Christian discipleship. Where Mary is, there is the Pentecostal breath of the Holy Spirit; there is new beginning and authentic renewal."

—**Pope Benedict XVI**

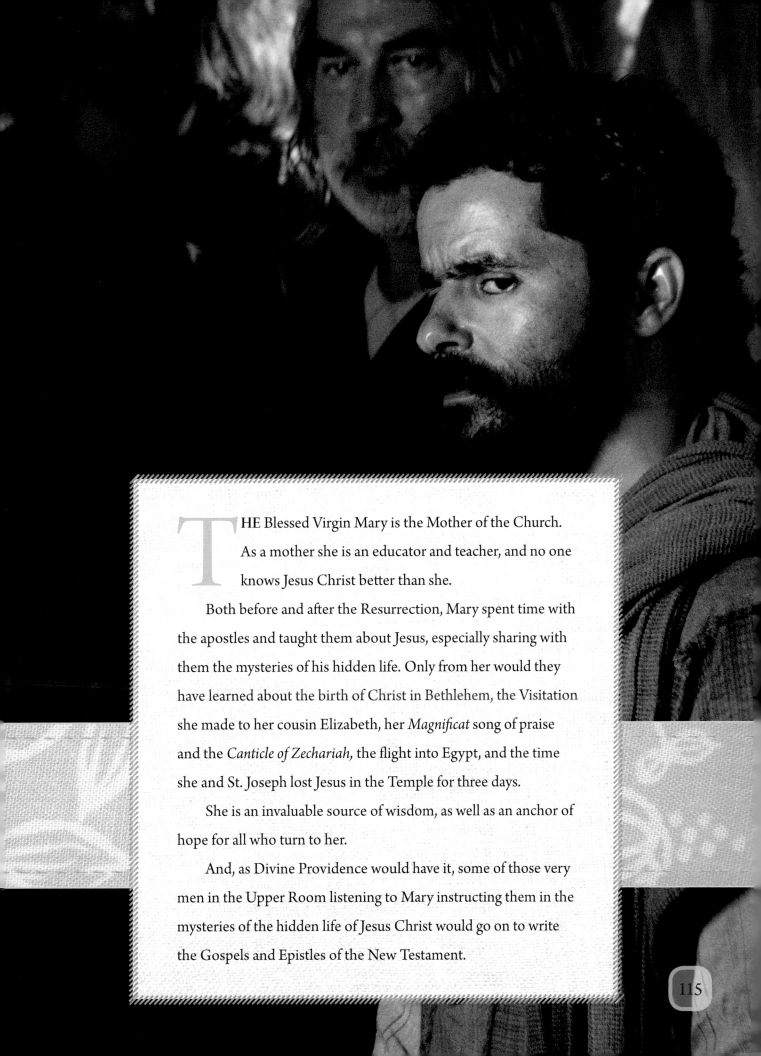

THE Blessed Virgin Mary is the Mother of the Church. As a mother she is an educator and teacher, and no one knows Jesus Christ better than she.

Both before and after the Resurrection, Mary spent time with the apostles and taught them about Jesus, especially sharing with them the mysteries of his hidden life. Only from her would they have learned about the birth of Christ in Bethlehem, the Visitation she made to her cousin Elizabeth, her *Magnificat* song of praise and the *Canticle of Zechariah,* the flight into Egypt, and the time she and St. Joseph lost Jesus in the Temple for three days.

She is an invaluable source of wisdom, as well as an anchor of hope for all who turn to her.

And, as Divine Providence would have it, some of those very men in the Upper Room listening to Mary instructing them in the mysteries of the hidden life of Jesus Christ would go on to write the Gospels and Epistles of the New Testament.

"If we have a box in which we keep our money, we know that one thing we must always give attention to is the key; we never think that the key is the money, but we know that without the key we cannot get our money. Our Blessed Mother is like the key. Without her we can never get to Our Lord, because he came through her. She is not to be compared to Our Lord, for she is a creature and he is the Creator. But if we lose her, we cannot get him. That is why we pay so much attention to her; without her we could never understand how that bridge was built between heaven and earth."

—Venerable
Fulton J. Sheen

A S IT was in the Old Testament, where the queen was the mother of the king and interceded for the people, so it is in the New Testament of Our Lord Jesus Christ. Mary is the heavenly Queen who sits at the right hand of the King of glory.

Jesus has assumed his Mother into the realm of heaven, body and soul, to sit at his right hand forever. Never again will they be separated; never again will they be apart.

Because Jesus lives, Mary lives. And she lives to intercede for his people. She lives to bring all people to Jesus. She is the Mother of God and our spiritual Mother.

She is Mary of Nazareth.

Pope Benedict XVI on Mary of Nazareth *by Anthony J. Ryan*

POPE Benedict XVI watched *Mary of Nazareth* in the Apostolic Palace in May 2012. At the end of the screening, the Pope addressed a few words on the film that focused on the three female protagonists: Herodias, Mary Magdalene, and Mary of Nazareth, whose lives cross but who choose very different paths.

"Herodias," Benedict XVI said, "remains locked within herself and her world. She is unable to raise her gaze to read the signs from God and she is not freed from evil. Mary Magdalene's experience is more complicated. She is attracted by the appeal of an easy life rooted in material things and uses various means for getting her own way up until the dramatic moment when she is judged and is faced with her own life. Her encounter with Jesus opens her heart and changes her existence."

Benedict was clearly touched by the portrayal of Mary. "But the center is Mary of Nazareth who possesses the wealth of a life that has been a 'Here I am' for God. She is a mother who would have always wanted to keep her son at her side, but she knows that he is God. Her faith and her love are so great that she can accept him leaving to accomplish his mission. Her life is a constant 'Here I am', said to God from the Annunciation until the Cross."

"Three experiences", the Pope concluded, "a paradigm of how one can build their life around selfishness, being locked within oneself and material things, being guided by evil, or rather upon the presence of a God who came and stays with us, who awaits us with kindness if we make a mistake and asks that we follow him, that we trust in him. Mary of Nazareth is the woman of a full and total 'Here I am' to the divine will. In her 'Yes', repeated even when faced with the sorrow of the loss of her child, we find complete and profound beatitude."

Notes from Film Director Giacomo Campiotti

by Anthony J. Ryan

THE director of *Mary of Nazareth*, Giacomo Campiotti, offered some interesting insights and background to the making of this epic film in an extended conversation with Ignatius Press. Campiotti, a well-respected veteran filmmaker (*Bakhita, Dr. Zhivago, St. Giuseppe Moscati*), worked with a very talented team of people in the movie industry, including accomplished screenwriter Francesco Arlanch (*Restless Heart, Pius XII, Pope John Paul II*) and a large cast from several countries. Although it is primarily an Italian-produced film, he said they did the casting for roles not only in Rome but in Paris, London, and Berlin as well.

Regarding making this movie, Campiotti reflected, "For me it has been a big gift and a great honor working on this film project. In preparation, I of course read the four gospels and have been struck again by their power and clarity. I also read the writings of German mystic Anne Catherine Emmerich (*The Life of the Blessed Virgin Mary*). Her visions and insights had more impact on me than history books or theological books that I have also read. I took from them some of the most intense images that I tried to realize in the movie." (Mel Gibson also drew from the writings and visions of Emmerich for scenes in his movie *The Passion of the Christ*.)

Campiotti explained that his goal for the film was to tell the truth about Mary, a unique person in history, and he wanted to convey her humanity and humility, as well as her deep faith and trust in God and in the great mysteries that she was asked to believe and live. He hoped to portray her as the loving Mother of the man Jesus, the wife of Joseph, and also the holy Mother of God. He noted that it was important to him to show Mary as a very real person, who in her freedom chose to follow the path God called her to, always striving to make herself open to his will in all the choices she made in her life, no matter how small. Campiotti used the theme of "Here I am" for Mary in the film to depict this attitude of openess to God's will for her. He said it was also crucial to show the deep joy that Mary had, even in the midst of the great challenges and sufferings she faced.

"Choosing the cast for this movie was delicate and difficult", said Campiotti. Most challenging was finding the right actress to play Mary, a role for which he auditioned many actresses from several different countries. They finally found a French actress that he and his crew thought was the best choice. But then he received a self-made video audition by a German actress he did not know, Alissa Jung. She was about to leave for Haiti to work on

her nonprofit organization that she had founded (*Pen Paper Peace*) to build schools for the poorest children there, when her agent begged her to audition for the role. Since she was leaving for Haiti, she only had time to make a video of herself reading some of the script on her home computer and e-mail it to Rome. Campiotti was struck by her simplicity, peacefulness, and goodness, and he had her come to Rome to audition in person after she returned from Haiti. Once he saw her in person, he became immediately convinced that Alissa was the right actress to play this key role in the film. Jung said that she was surprised and deeply honored to win the role of someone as great as Mary, especially as such a last-minute candidate.

Describing Alissa, Campiotti explained, "She made Mary a real woman, humble but also strong and joyful, profound, and aware of her great vocation. In her real life Alissa has two kids, and this 'maternal knowledge' gives Mary a familiar tenderness, but never sentimental."

Another big challenge for Campiotti was to find the right person to play Jesus. He again saw many auditions but couldn't find what he wanted. "Then during the casting for the role of Joseph in Berlin, we found Andreas Pietschmann", he said. "I asked him right away to change character and try the role of Jesus, and he did the lines of the Sermon on the Mount, 'The Beatitudes'. In his eyes I found the kindness and the power of love that we were looking for in Jesus." As it turned out, both lead roles were won by Germans.

Campiotti remarked that he was very pleased and fortunate to also have found such talented actors for the other major roles: Luca Marinelli as Joseph, Paz Vega as Mary Magdalene, and Antonia Liskova as Herodias. He was very impressed and grateful by how professional and committed the actors all were to this film, working long and continuous days without any complaints, but rather offering positive suggestions and helpful ideas for the film. He noted that there was a real spirit of family and friendship among this cast and crew, and he felt that bond of unity was reflected in the spirit and quality of the film. In addition to the actors, he said the technical crew

was also outstanding, including the photography, sound, editing, costumes, sets, and the lovely music score by Guy Farley.

Campiotti expressed his hope that, through this film, "Mary can be an example of love, faith, and strength for women today, especially young women. Mary was very brave, especially when she was so young and no one believed her; yet she continued to follow the path God called her to. Young people today need this deep message of love in a cynical world. Mary is a strong model for them that there is a much deeper meaning to life than the materialism of our culture."

Concluding, Campiotti said he is privileged to be able to make films, and he believes that movies can have a huge impact for good in our culture. "There is a great spiritual power in making movies," he noted. And his goal is only to make movies that tell uplifting stories with strong spiritual and human values that reflect the dignity of the human person. "Life is a miracle that comes from God."

Bibliography

Pope Benedict XVI, Maria: *On the Mother of God.* San Francisco: Ignatius Press, 2009.

Calloway, Donald H., MIC. *Marian Gems: Daily Wisdom on Our Lady.* Stockbridge, Mass.: Marian Press, 2014.

Calloway, Donald H., MIC. *Under the Mantle: Marian Thoughts from a 21st Century Priest.* Stockbridge, Mass.: Marian Press, 2013.

Calloway, Donald H., MIC, ed. *The Virgin Mary and Theology of the Body.* Stockbridge, Mass.: Marian Press, 2005.

The Holy Bible. Revised Standard Version. Second Catholic Edition. San Francisco: Ignatius Press, 2006.

Sheen, Fulton J. *The World's First Love.* San Francisco: Ignatius Press, 1996.

Library of Congress Control Number 2014947771
ISBN 978-1-58617-998-4

Published by:
Ignatius Press
www.ignatius.com

Printed and bound in the United States of America